# Wanderers in Northampton
# The Second Journey

*Following further in the steps of George Harrison,*
*artist, writer and poet (1876-1950)*

by

John and Vera Worledge

Meridian Books

Published 1994 by Meridian Books

© John and Vera Worledge 1994

ISBN 1-869922-24-7

Meridian Books
40 Hadzor Road
Oldbury
Warley
West Midlands
B68 9LA

Printed in Great Britain by BPC Wheatons Ltd., Exeter.

# Contents

*The Lodges, Ashby St. Ledgers (Trail 1)*

# Introduction.

In this second volume of *Wanderers in Northamptonshire* we follow further in the footsteps of George Harrison. By trade a hairdresser, he was a skilled artist and poet who had studied art in Brussels and who soon attracted the attention of the Kettering artist, Sir Alfred East R.A. His work was regularly shown in the annual Kettering Art Exhibition, of which he was at one time the secretary, and at a number of other important exhibitions.

Landscapes were his especial interest and his great love of the Northamptonshire countryside resulted in a series of descriptive articles, pen and ink sketches, and poems, that appeared regularly during the 1920s, '30s and '40s in the *Kettering Leader* and in other local newspapers. A collection of these was published in his book *A Wanderer in Northamptonshire* and it was through a discovery of this book, long out of print, that we first learned of his work. We are delighted that the response to our first volume of *Wanderers in Northamptonshire* has resulted in many more readers being introduced to his work.

George Harrison visited and wrote about so many places in Northamptonshire that we could not include them all in the first book so this second volume became necessary.

George, apparently, did not write about the village of Helidon (*Trail 1*).

*John and Vera at Weston Favell Church*

J Sainsbury Staff Magazine

However, we found it to be a haven of tranquillity where we met such a friendly group of people that we felt it should be included.

We have also included the Soke of Peterborough (*Trail 10*). In George's time it formed part of Northamptonshire although boundary changes have placed it today in Cambridgeshire – not, we thought, a reason for its exclusion.

Again we would like to dedicate this book to our lovely grandchildren, Katy and George; to Dorothy Webb, Mary Exley and Joan Carnell, the granddaughters of George Harrison; and to Aunt Renée, aunt to George's granddaughters.

John and Vera Worledge.

*The Old Farmyard, Winter*

# George Harrison's reminiscences of his younger days

### from his book

### A Wanderer in Northamptonshire

MY birthplace was the old Workhouse Lane, Kettering, in a cottage where now stands the building of the Northamptonshire Printing and Publishing Co. At the back of the cottage was the wood yard with its sawyers pit, and at the bottom lived Arch, the carrier. Near here, too, Meadows had his bake house. Soon my people moved to Rockingham Road.

I remember as a boy, how, during the long summer evenings, the shadows of the sails from the old windmill used to pass over the shop window; and late in the autumn I have seen the corn harvested in the fields, where now stands the playground of the council school. A green led from Rockingham Road to the old mill, with the mill house and the buildings to the left. This was a typical country lane, where elderberry bushes grew on either side, and wild roses trailed in profusion amidst tall trees with a view of the mill beyond. It was painted by all artists of that time because of its rural simplicity and picturesque composition. I used to play on the grass opposite the mill, where now is Regent Street, and a walk to Milestone Lane (now Britannia Lane) used to seem a long way into the country in those days. In this lane, on the right hand side from Rockingham Road, was a pond partly hidden by willow and ash trees, which was a hunting ground for tiddlers whenever I had the courage to walk thus far.

The first school I attended was that of an old lady of the name of Brigstock, who lived in a cottage, one of a number under the name of Uppingham Terrace, opposite the shop in Rockingham Road. This old lady did little more than act as a nurse for small children. She would keep us quiet, I well remember, by scooping out with an old bone scoop the centre of an apple which she ate with evident relish, giving the best behaved child the rind.

After this I was sent to Gold Street which was at that time the infant department of the British School, under Miss Clark. The British School had overgrown its space, and this room was leased from the deacons of Fuller Church to relieve the congestion. Thus we boys and girls used to play in Sally Croft's entry, much to the annoyance of the old lady, who would chase us away with a broom. Arthur Studd had his foundry at the top of the entry, and Mr. Walter Bell a corn chandler's shop at the bottom, where he followed Mr James, a furniture dealer. Mrs Smith kept a small shop opposite the school on the top of a number of steps, where I am afraid most of our halfpennies went in the purchase of delectable treacle toffee. At Fuller Church there was a splendid lending library, which was a real acquisition to us boys who early cultivated a love of good reading. I can still see those books, carefully covered with black cotton material, the work of the Misses Goodfellow. It was a real joy to go down to the library on a Saturday afternoon and select a book for the following week. Even now I marvel at the broad outlook of those people, who did not confine their selection of works to a kind which would repel, rather than encourage the love of reading. Mrs Henry Wood's works, I remember, were very much in favour, also the Brontë's, while books of travel were numerous and carefully selected, as were the works of eminent divines.

I was taken by my father to see Charles Bradlaugh who came to Kettering on the eve of the school board election. He was met and taken round the town in a procession headed by men carrying torches, and afterwards spoke at the Corn Exchange. My father told me to stand under the lamp which was in the centre of the Market Hill, so that he could find me when the meeting was over. The doors of the Corn Exchange were wide open owing to the large crowd, and I could distinctly hear Bradlaugh's voice, which, as many will remember, was of great volume and purity.

At this time I was at the British School, in School Lane, under Mr. Arthur Lenton, whose teaching was thorough, although his methods were severe. When I think of the conditions then prevailing I marvel that any results of value were possible. The crowded classrooms were filled with boys and girls, not always of the same age, and the rooms were uncomfortable during summertime and cold and ill-ventilated during the winter months. The curriculum was limited in scope, but what the teachers did have to teach, they were determined should be driven home in a manner too well impressed ever to be forgotten by the scholars for the rest of our lives. The playgrounds were very inadequate, which meant that before and after school hours most of the play took place in the street, entailing a good deal of clashing between the boys from the British School and the boys from the National School in the Horsemarket, then under the mastership of Mr S. J. Harding. These encounters became somewhat strenuous at times — particularly when snow was about — with resultant disfigurements to many on both sides.

Still, looking back to those days I recall that we were very happy and contented. We knew nothing of better schools, and certainly did not visualise the perfectly

*A photograph taken c. 1920 at the opening of the annual Kettering Art Exhibition. George Harrison (clearly the only hairdresser among them!) is standing on the right at the back, next to fellow Kettering artist J. Alfred Gotch.*

healthy conditions of the schools today. Most men of mature age remember the excellent results reflected in the afterlife of those who were fortunate enough to attend the British School. The conditions were bad, utterly bad, but by some means I have never quite understood, the results came, and these in larger proportion than in other bigger and better equipped schools.

I was in my thirteenth year when I left the British School, and then came the urge to draw and to paint. I was put in the hairdresser's shop where I had to stay until nine o'clock most days and eleven or eleven thirty on Saturdays. At this time there were no early closing days, but at every opportunity — mostly in the early mornings during spring and summer — I found my way into the country. This laid the foundation of my love for, and the familiarity with, my own county.

It was at this time that Sir Alfred East, T. C. Gotch and J. T. Nettleship, all of Kettering, were becoming famous in the art world. I was privileged to go often to see Sir Alfred East, who had a London studio in Spencer Street off Victoria Street,

*The River Nene in Spring*

near the new Westminster Cathedral. My first visit was just after he had returned from Japan. He was holding a most successful exhibition of his Japanese drawings in Bond Street, where every individual drawing found a ready purchaser. Mr T. C. Gotch often dropped in to see me when he was visiting Kettering and it was through his influence, and the kindly help of Mr Frank Berrill (Manager of the Midland Bank) and of Mr Charles Henson that I was able to go to Antwerp in company with the late W. B. Gash, my first art master, where we spent the summer in hard and continuous study.

The years have rolled away in happy and continuous work. Many changes have come to Kettering, but more have come to the countryside immediately surrounding it. The necessity of widening roads, and the making of arterial roads, the sin of ribbon building, and the felling of much fine timber without replanting has played sad havoc with parts of the county — the county that inspired Sir Alfred East and T. C. Gotch and laid foundation for their art. Sometimes I feel depressed regarding the future; at other times I have faith that good sense will prevail, and schemes of development be put forward, so that the county will move along the road of progress, maintaining the loveliness which has been an inspiration to so many in the past.

If strong public opinion is maintained, I see no reason why the county should not remain beautiful for all time, an inspiration to our people, and a joy in its beholding — a place of quiet peace, and fruitful toil, and where the aged may rest, and the children grow up in happy anticipation of healthy, good lives.

George Harrison. 1945.

## Contents of the first volume of Wanderers in Northamptonshire

# THE NENE VALLEY.

### By GEORGE HARRISON.

I LOVE these meadows, cool and sweet,
 That lie so near to broad highway,
Where drooping pollard willows meet
And shimmer in the light of day.
I love the river, flowing by
 Tall flags and plumy-headed reeds,
The flowers that match the hue of sky,
Those pure delights misnamed as weeds.

Here through the warm September noon
 I linger idly and content,
And feel the sun a pleasant boon.
Though summer days be well nigh spent
I see the leaves to russet turn,
 They flutter light as fairy wings,
The hawthorn buds with crimson burn,
Where perky robin sits and sings.

Beyond the river, gently rise
 Those truant paths that winding, go
By lofty trees to meet the skies,
With half the green world spread below,

Strange how the changing colours blend,
 Through wooded depths and leafy lea,
With melting hues that have no end,
To glimmer like the restless sea.

Grey farms and hamlets nestle down
 By labyrinths of oak and fir,
By little fields of gold and brown
 Light floating films of gossamer,
That brightly beam, or fade from view
 When clouds obscure the glowing sun,
With trailing shadows softly blue
 Which pass away when scarce begun.

And seated here a tender joy
 Comes to me sweet with odours blown,
Unfettered and without alloy,
 By beauty born from beauty's throne,
And all I ask for still abides
 In flowering meads, and vaulted dome
Of tender blue where white cloud rides
 Above the scenes I name my home.

*One of George Harrison's original contributions to*
*the Kettering and Northamptonshire Advertiser*

# Acknowledgements

We wish to record our grateful thanks to the following for their help in the compilation of both volumes of *Wanderers in Northamptonshire*.

Neil Griffin, whose chance remark at a photography class led us to our trails around the county;

The Northampton and Kettering libraries for their extensive help in the tracing of George Harrison's granddaughters;

Simon Thortons (Jewellers) of Kettering for their help with the addresses of the granddaughters;

Joan Carnell, Mary Exley and Dorothy Webb, the granddaughters of George Harrison, who gave us permission to use George's works in our book;

The staff of the Kettering Art Gallery for showing us the paintings by George that are stored and displayed at the gallery;

Malcolm Robinson of the Kettering Reference Library for his unstinting help in discovering notes on George in the reference library;

The Editors of the *Kettering Leader and Telegraph* and *The Citizen*, and to Carmel Crawley of the Archive Department, for their help and permission to publish George's work for the papers from the 1930s and the 1940s;

Jennifer Fell of Hellidon for her advice on our manuscript;

Ted Eassom of Rothwell for acquiring the 1928 poems and for his help in obtaining two of George's paintings;

The *Northampton Chronicle and Echo* newspapers for permission to publish (in the first volume) their photographs of the 800 year charter;

Rachel Watson, County Archivist, for her help with the Charter photostat and her advice in the preparation of our books;

Mrs Jean Holt of Harrington, who sent us a 1927 book of George's poems;

Edwin John Storry of Broughton who gave us a lovely pen and pencil sketch by George Harrison;

Mr John Thomas Neville R.I.B.A., who did the marvellous drawings of the architectural periods of our churches that appeared in the first volume;

Our dear friends at Corby, Georgina and Bernard Barry, for their gift of Nickolaus Pevsner's book of Northamptonshire;

Mrs Odell for her help with the initial photostats for our manuscript;

*Prontaprint* of Northampton for their help with the final photostats for our manuscript;

Northampton Record Society for information about the works of John Clare.

...and finally to the people of Northamptonshire who gave us so much help as we toured the county.

Vera and John Worledge

# Trail 1
## Flore • Newnham • Badby• Hellidon • Ashby St Ledgers • Naseby

## Flore

WE visited Flore in the summer of 1991 and immediately ran into a puzzle concerning a small thatched cottage known as Adams' Cottage. When we were delving in the archives we found a newspaper cutting from June 1921 which read:

### Village link with famous president
### Americans buy ancient Northants chapel
### Adams cottage

A fascinating story comes from Flore, a little village near Northampton, providing an historical link between the county and the United States.

In this typical English village is a tiny thatched cottage, with ancient lead-paned windows and yellowed plastered walls. For generations its been known as "Adams' Cottage" but why is it so called has been a mystery to most inhabitants.

Now, however, researches have proved that it has important associations with John Adams, the second President of the United States. His grandfather, the Rev. Thomas Adams, established a Quakers Meeting house there in 1662. He was ejected from his living for holding Puritan principles.

**Nameless graves**

The cottage remained as a Quaker's chapel from 1662 to 1781, and the names of 35 Quakers have been found in the Friends' register of Northampton and the Flore church register as having been buried in the old world garden attached to this cottage.

The first 21 on this list are named Adams, ancestors of the great American who succeeded Washington as President, but there is no headstone, no footstone and no memorial of any kind to mark their graves.

This once-hallowed ground is planted with vegetables, and the forebears of one who was America's chief citizen now sleeps in nameless graves beneath peas, potatoes, cabbages and fruit trees.

Besides the Adams family there are several relatives of the Pilgrim Fathers lying there.

The Sulgrave Institution in New York decided to buy the property in order to preserve it for the British nation. This was arranged, and the Americans propose to restore it to something like its original appearance as an old Quaker's meeting house.

Fortunately many of the ancient features of the place, including the cupboard over the windows where their bibles and hymn-books were stored, are still in existence, and the Institution appeals for the loan or purchase of the old Quaker's stools, forms and books, particulary those relics belonging to the Adams family.

*Adams' Cottage*

*The Old School House...*

In spite of having written to America, and delving in numerous archives and books, we have not yet been able to confirm who owns the property now. However, it seems that the American ownership was never established.

The Church of All Saints is partly thirteenth century with a massive fourteenth century tower. It has finely carved medieval doors and contains some good brasses. The sixteenth century font was, at one time, used as a cattle trough!

The school has now been tastefully converted to a private residence. We had to take our photograph from a different position because the view as George saw it is now obstructed by some new housing.

*...and the school as George saw it*

# Newham

*Set high upon a breezy hill,*
*With half the green world spread below,*
*The Newham cottages look down*
*On little paths that winding go*
*By beechen woods, the fields that rise*
*To meet the far clouds crown of snow.*

The Church of St Michael, Newnham

*The church is quite unchanged today*

FROM Flore we came to Newham, another delightful village, mostly of ironstone in the hilly country between Fawsley and Daventry. This was the birthplace of the Elizabethan poet Thomas Randolph; he lies at Blatherwyke where he died while visiting a friend.

The church entrance of St Michael is unique for you walk under the arched tower to gain entrance to the church. The tower is of the fourteenth century with a recessed spire, and there are attractive boxed pews in the aisles.

George visited Newham in 1929 as you can see from the date of his sketch.

According to the historical notes on the village in Whellan's *History, Gazetteer & Directory* of 1849 the church was at that time dedicated to the Blessed Virgin, but whether or not that was a misprint we never found out.

# Badby

HERE we find another beautiful village located in the uplands of Northamptonshire. George wrote:

From Newham we follow the lane to the main road and cross the river to Badby, which rises above the stripling Nene only a mile or two from its source, near Staverton. It is a lovely village, especially at bluebell time. We climb up towards the church, and near it find the quaint Round House, probably at some period a toll-gate house.

From near the church there is a glorious view over high-lying, wooded country, with Arbury Hill, the highest point in the county, rising 735 feet above sea level. The hill is crowned with earth works similar to those which lie along the face of the Cotswolds, for the Nene has brought us from the fenlands to the limestone heights on the scarp of which we could walk almost to Bristol.

I was visiting the village doing a County Trail quiz for BBC Radio Northampton and Mrs Hartshorne, who lives opposite the church, showed me round the

*The Round House, Badby*

church and switched on the church bells for me to record for the programme. Her husband had electrified the bells so they struck just by pressing a switch – a fine bit of electrical engineering!

The Lantern House, or Round House, on the edge of the woods is of the early nineteenth century and is now a private residence. It had become derelict but was tastefully restored in 1972. The door lintel is dated 1981 indicating some further renovation.

*...and George's sketch*

In the summer of 1991 we ventured into the woods above the village to find the Dower House in Fawsley Park – a lovely walk especially during bluebell time. While we were walking in the woods we were told that a black bear had been seen in the woods that summer. We kept a wary eye open but saw nothing!

*In Badby Woods*

## Hellidon

ALTHOUGH George apparently never visited this delightful place, situated in the Northamptonshire uplands and, so far undisturbed, we love it so much that we could not miss it out. Also we like the following story of the honey bees of St John the Baptist Church.

*The bells before being sent for recasting*

During the second world war church bells were not allowed to be rung, being saved to warn the general public of a German invasion of Britain. But after the great victory in the North African desert Winston Churchill decreed that the British public should celebrate and the order went out to ring all the church bells. However, when the bell ringers went to the tower of St John the Baptist all the ropes were stuck fast. So up the belfry they went, only to find that bees had built their nest among the works and a very substantial amount of honey had jammed the bells!

While in the village we met a delightful lady, Jennifer Fell, who had already written an excellent book on Hellidon (well worth a read) and helped us very

*Hellidon Church*

much in compiling our manuscript. We made several delightful visits to the village (with excellent meals in the local hostelry) and met the people of the village at a fête to celebrate the 400 year consecration of the church.

Following on from the story of the bells, Jenifer invited John over on 20th. September 1993 to see the bells being taken down to be sent to the Whitechapel Foundry in London for repair. This work was all completed by volunteers from the village.

When they were brought down it was discovered that they were all engraved in Latin; one was

*One of the James I coins discovered on the Hellidon bells*

dedicated to Charles I, and one was dated 1635. One bell had three coins braized onto the bell, and after some concerted cleaning the head of James I appeared together with the numerals XII denoting the twelfth year of his reign.

The peal of four bells was first hung in 1615 and 1635 and rehung in 1860.

If you look on both sides of the church porch you will see large groove marks: according to legend these marks were made by soldiers from the parliamentarian armies sharpening their swords before going to battle in the Civil War, probably at Edgehill in 1642.

## *Ashby St Ledgers*

Before entering Ashby St Ledgers from Welton we pass through leafy lanes which are as picturesque as in any county. There is a charm in the approach to most villages – at a bend in the road, perhaps where one first sees the church spire or tower above the trees. The quickness of a car in reaching one's destination not always compensates for missing the cottage gardens, where, with a more leisurely approach, one catches the fragrance of flowers, the scent of the wood fires from the chimneys and the sense of calm, of rural simplicity ... The trees are breaking into leaf, every garden is gay with spring flowers. In the tall elm trees the noisy rooks are busy with their clamorous broods, and everywhere the songs of birds rise and fall on the varying breeze. The westering sun is gilding the tower of the church, and long shadows are thrown on the lush grass. Children are playing as only children can, when spring stars the meadows with flowers;the sounds of evening enfolds the earth, and a "peace that passeth all understanding" falls softly as on angels' wings.

WE followed George's advice and left our car outside the village. Here we are in one of the most famous villages in the county and the home of Sir Robert Catesby, the leading conspirator in the Gunpowder Plot. He brooded over the wrong-doings of the times and resolved to destroy both King and

*Church of St Leodegarius and Gate House, Ashby St Ledgers*

*The Gatehouse, meeting place of the Gunpowder Conspirators*

Parliament and establish a Catholic Government in their place. He met with his conspirators in the room over the gate-house at the Manor House at Ashby St Ledgers to hatch the plot. We have read several reports on the conspirator's plans and what follows is a collation of all those reports.

It was Robert Catesby who instigated the plot: he had been fined heavily for refusing to attend Protestant services and had to pay great sums of money to Francis Bacon, the corrupt Chancellor of the day. He was finally driven to sell his estates and move in with his mother at the Manor House at Ashby St Ledgers.

The plan was to put a mine under the House of Lords, the intention being to fire the mine when the King and both Houses were assembled, this date being November 5th 1605. A small building close to the House of Lords was acquired and the work of digging and cutting through solid stone was abandoned after a while as they found that they could gain access to the House of Lords through a maze of corridors beneath the house. Guy Fawkes was seized on November 4th as he was entering the cellars – this was due to an anonymous letter having been sent to one of the members of the House of Lords warning him not to attend as his life would be in mortal danger. (It was thought, but never proved, that Lord Tresham had sent the letter to one of his friends.)

The conspirators rode north with great haste to Ashby St Ledgers. Catesby rode a string of horses from London and arrived at the Manor House as Lady Catesby and her friends were sitting down to dinner. After a brief conference they decided to ride on to Wales, stopping overnight in a friend's house in

Holbeche in Staffordshire. There they were discovered and the house was surrounded by the local sheriff and his men. In the ensuing battle some gunpowder in the house was ignited and an explosion occurred setting fire to the house. As they fled the house they were cut down in a hail of bullets.

Linger awhile in this delightful spot and look round the lovely old church to see the marvellous three tier Jacobean pulpit, meander through the village and see the beautiful thatched cottages by Lutyens.

The Inn-cum-Post Office is also worth a visit. The Manor House at the time of writing is empty and the gate-house is in a dreadful state of disrepair. Let's hope that this piece of history is not lost forever.

*A Vista of Spring*

# Naseby

*The Welland and the Avon, crystal clear,*
*From bubbling springs commence their journeys here;*
*One flows through flow'ring fields its eastwards way,*
*By lofty elms and drooping willows grey;*
*The other, turning westwards from its source,*
*Meanders softly on its level course,*
*By Stratford, where the "Bard of Avon" sleeps,*
*To meet the Severn; the fair Malvern sweeps*
*Her rolling hills across the tranquil skies,*
*And Bredons breezy uplands gently rise.*

WE arrived on a fine summer's day, to photograph where George once sat, at a time when another battle was raging – not on the battlefield but in the High Court where an attempt was being made to get the Government to move the route of the A1-M1 link road so that it did not cross the famous Naseby Battlefield. Alas!, the attempt failed. So gaze on our photograph, a scene never to be the same again.

*Naseby*

It has been claimed that it was here that democracy was born, back in 1645, the year of the Battle of Naseby. The battle took place between the Royalists of Charles I and the Roundheads of Oliver Cromwell.

Here is George's account:

*The Monument on the Naseby Battlefield*

The campaign of Naseby began with the retreat of the Royal army from Borough Hill near Daventry towards Market Harborough. Fairfax, hot on their heels, slept the night at Guilsborough – this was the 13th. of June – and set off at 3 a.m. to bring the Royal troops to bay. A raid by Ireton's cavalry had surprised some of Rupert's troopers at Naseby on the evening before; this caused Rupert and Charles to turn back to meet the advancing army. Charles hoisted his flag on Moot Hill, near Sibbertoft; Rupert advanced through Clipston, and, mistaking the deployment of the parliamentary forces for a retreat, swept round their left wing, and drove all before him until he reached the parliamentary baggage train behind Naseby. Meanwhile Cromwell, who had arrived with his cavalry from Ely by forced marches, had wheeled in the flank of the advancing Royalists' centre, Charles' reserves failed to support and Rupert arrived too late to save the battle; though his infantry fought gallantly, the rest of the Royalist army fled into Leicestershire, but a large body was rounded up in the church yard at Marston Trussel, near the Northamptonshire border.

Naseby has another honour as being the source of the River Avon that flows through Stratford on its way to the Severn and the sea.

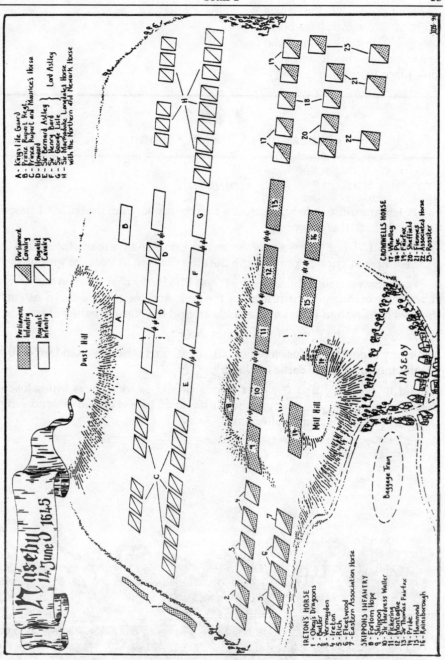

*The dispositions of the armies before the Battle of Naseby*

With grateful thanks to Barry Denton

# Trail 2
Sibbertoft • Clipston • Braunston

## *Sibbertoft*

IT IS perhaps difficult to believe today that the smoke from the Battle of Naseby once drifted over this village.

Sibbertoft Manor is now a private nursing home and we thank the staff of the home for permission to photograph the attractive scene from the grounds.

We made two delightful visits to Mr and Mrs Burton, who live in the village. They told us much of the history of the area, and their son showed us some musket balls he had found in the fields around the Naseby battlefield.

The source of the River Welland rises close by.

Nearby Moot Hill is close to where Charles Stuart raised his standard on that fateful morning of the Battle of Naseby.

Laid to rest here in 1889, after a long period as vicar, was Miles Joseph Berkeley who was also a famous botanist and an expert on mosses and fungi. A genus of algae is named after him.

*The Manor, Sibbertoft*

*Sibbertoft Manor is now a nursing home*

## Clipston

THIS village is known for its great flood of 1880 when on St Swithins day (15th July) a great storm swept over Northamptonshire and the flood water poured through the village sweeping all before it, including all the mud built dwellings (known as 'cob' dwellings). 'Cob' is, strictly speaking, a West

*The Green, Clipston*

Country word and describes a particular method of building with mud. Mud was, of course, very widely used in the early construction of farmhouses, cottages, barns and garden walls.

The walls were constructed of solid mud up to two feet thick and always built on a stone or brick base, normally about eighteen inches high. Frequently, chopped straw, grass and cow dung was added to strengthen the adhesion of the material. Cob walling was built up in layers in a damp state and had to set before the next layer was added – consequently the builders moved around the site adding layers as they dried out. You can see some of this work at Kilsby and Ravensthorpe. At Guilsborough there is a good example of a cob barn on the village green.

A couple of verses from George's poem on Clipston describes the peaceful village.

> Beyond the town, the road slopes down
> By lowland fields and pastures green,
> Then up to meet the rolling skies,
> Dappled with gold and blue between;
> A patterned film of colours spun
> By hue of clouds and glowing sun.
>
> Beneath the shade, by tall trees made,
> The white road winds through village street,
> By ancient church and cottage paths,
> With cobbles worn by toiling feet;
> Then, like a ribbon, rolls away
> To distant pine woods dim and grey.

*The Northamptonshire Uplands*

*Old Mill House in Braunston*

## *Braunston*

WE visited Braunston in the Summer of 1990 for the bi-centennial celebrations of the completion of the Oxford Canal. This was one of the earliest canals in the southern part of the country and although its building was authorised in 1769 it was not until 1790 that the line was completed. James Brindley, the great canal engineer, was originally engaged in its construction, but he died in 1772 and the work was taken over by Samuel Simcock.

The Grand Union and Oxford Canals meet at Braunston. There are extensive views over Warwickshire from the hill where the church of All Saints stands proud.

*Braunston Mill*

*Braunston*

On browsing through Whellan's *History, Gazetteer & Directory of Northamptonshire* of 1849 we came across the following passage:

*Mention is made in a charter of Edward III ... of a village or hamlet called Fawcliff, which stood to the north east of Braunston, but of which there are no present traces. Bridges describes a remarkable stone cross, 24ft. in height, which stood towards the upper end of town but which was levelled to the ground, and the material applied to the repair of the highways, many years since.*

*Preparing for Spring*

# Trail 3
Cosgrove • Fawsley • Preston Capes • Canons Ashby • Eydon

## *Cosgrove*

W E came to Cosgrove on a lovely sunny July day. In 1805 the canal reached the village which also became a junction of the canal to Buckingham, now abandoned. The area around the canal is attractive with a fine Gothic stone canal bridge dating from 1800 and recently restored (shown in our photograph), an interesting pedestrian tunnel under the canal, and the Georgian Cosgrove Hall overlooking the lock. Since George visited the area the gravel pits have been turned into a leisure park.

The rivers Ouse and Tove flow leisurely past: to the west of the village, on the canal, there is a marvellous piece of Victorian architecture, a cast iron aqueduct that carries the Grand Union Canal over the Ouse.

It seems that this was the result of the second attempt to bridge the river. It appears that the gap was first bridged in August 1805 on arches. The contractors guaranteed a trial of twelve months but before half that period had expired there was a big leak that flooded the surrounding countryside. They then built the cast iron aqueduct and this had lasted to the present day.

*The Canal Bridge at Cosgrove*

*The Church of Saints Peter and Paul, Cosgrove.*
*The figures are thought to be George's daughter Hilda and granddaughter Dorothy*

The church is dedicated to St Peter and St Paul and is the oldest building in the village. The chancel is twelfth century and although the chancel arch was damaged by fire in 1586 the remains of a medieval wall painting can still be seen on the wall above the arch.

*Our view of Cosgrove Church*

## Fawsley

THE home of the Knightleys, Fawsley Park and House are all that remains of the estate. The Hall has been empty for several years although we heard, when we last visited the park, that the present owner has had the Hall renovated.

*The Ruined Dower House, Fawsley*

*The Dower House has deteriorated further since George's time but at least the tower has been strengthened.*

The church in the grounds goes back to the Magna Carta. The estate was a little kingdom of its own, set in 300 acres of parkland (which you can drive through today and picnic in.)

The Hall was built by Edmond Knightley, who died in 1542, and was a member of a Puritan family.

George wrote:

The Great Hall at Fawsley is 43 feet high, and on its open timber roof of Irish bog-oak no spider has ever been known to spin its web.

The kitchens have a fine beamed ceiling, the bevelling of which is so similar to that in the grand hall at Sulgrave Manor as to make it likely that they are by the same hand. In the church, besides the rich heraldry of the Knightleys, are six armorial windows of the Washingtons rescued from Sulgrave Manor after it became a farmhouse. In the kitchen garden are quaint brick recesses for the old straw beehives of the seventeenth century.

The Dower House, built of brick and sandstone for a widow of the estate, probably around the same time as the Hall, was derelict as early as 1710. A plaque on the side of the house warns 'Ancient Monuments Act. Any persons, injuring or defacing this monument will be liable to prosecution according to law. Ministry of Works 1931'.

As you can see the tower is leaning, but recently it has been braced and underpinned to stop the lean. It is still a very worthwhile monument to save although, as you will see, we have lost quite a bit since George sat there to make his sketch.

## *Preston Capes*

THIS village nestles in the the countryside close to the Knightley estates and once formed part of them. There was a castle here in ancient times but today just the earthworks remain. It was the home of a French knight, Hugh de Capes.

*Old Cottages, Preston Capes*

Relics of the Knightleys hang in the church, a sword, a gauntlet and spurs: The iron-studded door is about 400 years old. The view sweeps sharply away from the west of the tower and gives you a magnificent view over Badby Woods and Fawsley Park together with views of Arbury and Borough hills and the Nene Valley by Newham. There is a lovely east window in the church – a visit to the village is worth while just to see this.

The Knightleys became good churchmen and Tories – in their long history fifteen took holy orders, and Sir Valentine was Rector of Preston Capes for 62 years. In 1898 Sir Valentine was succeeded in the baronetcy by Sir Charles Knightley, a veritable Sir Roger de Coverley, a man who lunched off bread and cheese, had regular hours when villagers or tenants could visit him, devoted himself to public work and was a keen follower of the Grafton and Pytchley hounds. His advice was sought from far and near on all public questions, and he exercised a most beneficial influence in the county for over thirty years.

*Preston Capes. The cottages today*

## Canons Ashby

THE church of St Mary is today only a fragment of its former glory and only the tower and the two arches of the aisle remain. However, these have been tastefully restored as has the whole area around the church.

The Elizabethan Country House is now owned by the National Trust and is open to the public at certain times. It was in the ownership of the Drydens for a long period and was still in private hands when George sketched his scene. The poet Edmund Spenser is thought to have written part of *The Fairie Queene* in the house, which contains a room named after him. In the following century the youthful John Dryden came and made friends with his pretty cousin Honor Dryden.

In 1551 John Dryden bought the land and buildings from the Black Augustian Monks of Canons Ashby, but it took until 1710 for the building to reach its present state. The gardens overlook the old deer park. In the great hall is the armour used on the Parliamentry side during the Civil War. If you look carefully at the tower of the church you will find it pitted with bullet marks from the Royalist's guns.

George wrote:

The Dryden home was begun in the 1550s but the tower belonged to a pre-Reformation building. John Dryden's son, Sir Erasmus, continued to build, and the house assumed its present form in 1710, since when it has been scarcely touched, except by the skillful hand of J.A. Gotch. It is an exquisite example of the old English home. The sketch shows the Garden Front and Green Court, which the latter opens into the deer park.

*Canons Ashby House*

*... is little changed today*

# *Eydon*

A LOVELY VILLAGE to visit with many buildings of beautiful brown stone. It suffered a devastating fire in 1651 and is now a conservation area.

Stone was once quarried here and was presumably used in the local buildings. To quote from Whellan's *Gazetteer* of 1849:

'*Here is excellent stone for building purposes, and Redwell, one of the principal springs*

*The Stocks, Eydon*

*The new trees around the stocks were planted for
the Silver Jubilee of Queen Elizabeth II*

in the area is chalybeate. *The Roman road from Bennaventa or Issannavaria to Brinavis
passed through this parish.'*

The church of St Nicholas, heavily restored in 1864-5 by R.C. Hussey, is well
worth a visit with its little squat tower. Look out for the house opposite the
green with its fine mullion windows. The stocks that George sketched are still
here although the elms have long since gone.

*Hay Harvest*

# Trail 4
### Aynho • Hinton in the Hedges • Sulgrave

## Aynho

AYNHO is the most southerly village in Northamptonshire and has a strong Cotswold influence. It is on a hill from which there are beautiful views of the surrounding Northamptonshire and Oxfordshire countryside. It is still known as the 'Apricot Village' after the trees that were planted against the houses in the village by the then Lords of the Manor, the Cartwrights. In past times it seems that tenants paid part of their rent in apricots, almost all houses having an apricot tree against them. The Aynho House nursery kept trees to replace dead or diseased trees, the local variety being named 'Moor Park'.

The majority of monuments in the village Church of St Michael are to the Cartwrights. Sadly Lord Cartwright and his only son and heir were tragically killed in a car crash in 1954 (this was after George made his visit). Although Elizabeth Cartwright-Hignett was a descendant she never stayed at the house after the accident and the estate was sold to a housing association and tastefully turned into apartments. Elizabeth wrote a charming book called *Lili at Aynhoe*, a story of her great-great-grandmother who came to England in 1828 as the wife of Sir Thomas Cartwright. She was a prolific artist and the book is full of her

*Aynho, the southernmost village in the County*

paintings of the rooms at Aynho during the period she lived there.

The Cartwrights were on the Parliamentary side during the Civil War. Their home and the body of the church was burnt down by the Royalists in their retreat from the Naseby battlefield. This explains why the Church of St Michael is of two periods – the tower dates from the fifteenth century but the body of

*George's scene today*

*Some of the apricot trees*

the church was rebuilt from 1723 to 1725 by Edward Wing, being designed to blend in with the style of the Manor House. If you look carefully around the village you will still see apricot trees growing up the walls of some of the houses.

Some years ago an Apricot Festival was held in the village when all the villagers helped collect the harvest from the trees.

## Hinton in the Hedges

THE church in this charmingly named village is dedicated to the Holy Trinity. It has a Norman tower and there is a lovely tomb inside the church to Sir

*At Hinton in the Hedges*

special about the local hedges: indeed the village was known as Hynton in the Edge in 1549 – the present name was in use by 1754.

The Crewe Inn in the village is named after Sir Thomas Crewe, a speaker of the House of Commons who died in 1634 and who lies interned in the private chapel in Steane Park, a few miles down the road.

This peaceful village nestles in the countryside close to Brackley, with no main road. We visited it on a lovely sunny Sunday afternoon in August 1991 when John did a 'County Trail' for BBC Radio Northampton. This took the form of a competition in which we toured four villages around the county giving clues to where we were – the listeners then had to guess where we finished up, how many miles we had covered and, using the letters in the names of the villages, to make a word from a cryptic clue that we gave them.

*Cottage in Duck Lane. We could find no signs of the duck pond shown in George's picture but hope this might be one of his thatched cottages*

# Sulgrave

WE came here on a hot sunny Sunday just after harvest time in 1991 for a tour of Sulgrave Manor. The Manor was first mentioned in the Domesday Book of 1086: it eventually came into the hands of the Crown and was sold by Henry VIII to Lawrence Washington who built the present fine house. His descendants lived here for 120 years until 1610 when financial circumstances forced them to leave and the manor was sold to one Laurence Makepeace, a gentleman of the Inner Temple, London. The second son of Laurence Washington, John Washington, emigrated to America in 1656 where he settled

*Sulgrave Manor, 1921 – 1929*

*(The remant of the Washington home as restored by the British people; later the West Wing was rebuilt, the North Wing restored, the grounds enlarged and the whole endowed mainly by the generosity of the National Society of Colonial Dames of America, a body which aims to perpetuate the fine qualities of Colonial America.)*

in Mount Vernon, Virginia. He was the grandfather of George Washington, first President of the United States of America. Not surprisingly Sulgrave Manor is a popular place of pilgrimage for visiting Americans.

The manor house was extensively restored and reopened on 21 June 1929 as a museum to the Washington family. A bust of George Washington was unveiled by Mr. John Stewart, Chairman of the Sulgrave Institution of America. In June 1924 several pieces of Washington artifacts were given to the manor by

*Sulgrave Manor, now restored*

the Sulgrave Institute of America, including saddle bags and a liquor chest used
by George Washington in the American Civil War, parchment deeds on
Sulgrave Manor, a coffin handle from the coffin in which George Washington
was buried and a section of the Washington Elm from Cambridge,
Massachusetts.

The house, which is open to the public, is beautifully furnished in period style
and has a fascinating fully equipped
eighteenth century kitchen. The gardens
are especially attractive with a sixteenth
century sundial in the Rose Garden.

The Church of St James in the village is
mostly fourteenth century but there is
some Saxon influence as suggested by the
west door. It still contains the Washington family pew. An iron chest is said to
have stored the loot of the infamous Cul-
worth gang of highwaymen and
cut-throats.

The following notes are by George:

John Washington, who went to Virginia
late in 1656, became Colonel John Washington, great grandfather of George
Washington, first President of the United
States of America. John Washington did not
leave England from Northamptonshire, but
his family had for four generations been
living in the county, and his father and
mother were both born and brought up

*The Arms of Lawrence Washington,
builder of Sulgrave Manor and
mayor of Northampton*

*The Bookplate of George Washington*

*(Note the absence of the crescent from the Arms)*

there. The family line runs back through the Wasshintons of Warton, Lancashire to the de Wessingtons of County Durham, one of whom, Sir Walter de Wessington, fought at the battle of Lewes in 1246. The Arms borne by George Washington and used in his bookplate occur in Lancashire documents of the early fifteenth century, and are carved on Warton church tower. From the 1530s to the 1600s, however, the great President's ancestors or their near relatives were living in Northamptonshire, and held an honourable position in county life. Their arms are seen in Northampton Town Hall, at Sulgrave Church and Manor, at Brington, Thrapston, Fawsley and at Weston Hall.

It is worth mentioning here that a number of prominent English writers have endeavoured to trace the origin of the United States flag to the design of the Washington Coat of Arms. Although George Washington kept minute diaries and was a voluminous letter writer, he makes no mention of the subject, nor do any of his contemporaries; and the version of his arms in his bookplate has no resemblance to the original 'Stars and Stripes' in which thirteen white stars were grouped in a constellation of stars, but the thirteen stripes, with the Union Jack (less St Patrick's Cross) in a canton, were on the 'Cambridge Flag' raised by George Washington at his Headquarters at Cambridge, Massachusetts on January 2nd, 1776.

It is not certain how long Laurence Washington resided in Brington. Tradition associates with him the homely dwelling seen in the picture of Little Brington, but partly obscured by a cart. It is a thatched house of brown ironstone, with square stone windows, but the interior woodwork is of fine quality. It was built in 1606. In 1899 a sundial bearing the date 1617 and carved with Robert Washington's Arms and initials. (*See Trail 9, Little Brington, for the sad story of the house.* ) This was found near the house; it has been set up at Althorp, and a copy, given to the State of Massachusetts by Earl Spencer, is in the State House, Boston, Mass. It is possible that Robert resided here as well as in the house with an inglenook, now divided into two cottages, which tradition allots to him in Great Brington.

*Elizabethan child's shoe, found at Sulgrave Manor*

# The Washington Genealogical Tree.

John Washington of Warton, Lancs = Margaret,da.of Robert Kytson of Warton
(15th century) Hall and aunt to Dame Katherine
Spencer of Althorp

(1) Elizabeth,widow of = Lawrence Washington = (2) Amee, da.of Robert
William Gough Lord of the Manor of Pargiter of Greatworth,
Sulgrave;b.c.1500 Northants, d.1564
d.1583-4

(1) Elizabeth,da. and heir = Robert Washington = (2) Anne Fisher of
of Walter Light of Lord of the Manor of Hanslope Bucks.
Radway, Warwicks Sulgrave; b.1540;
d 1619

Lawrence Washington of Sulgrave; b. = Margaret, eldest da. of William Butler of
c.1568 d.1616 buried at Brington Tighes, Sussex;m. 1588.
Northants.

Rev. Laurence Washington MA, BD, = Amphillys, da. of John Twigden of
Fellow of Brasenose College Oxford, Spratton Northants.
Rector of Purleigh, Essex, 1633-43;
d. Jan 1652-3

Colonel John Washington b. 1632 or = Anne, da. of Lieut Colonel Nathanial
3, settled in Virginia; d. Sept.1677 Pope.

Captain Lawrence Washington of = Mildred Warner
Virginia, d. 1697-8

(1) Jane Butler = Captain Augustine = (2) Mary Ball, A
Washington of descendant of the Ball
Virginia,1694-1743 family of Northants.
England.

General George Washington = Martha, widow of Daniel Parke Custis and
b. 11 Feb.1732; d. without issue da. of John Dandridge.
14 Dec.1799
FIRST PRESIDENT OF THE UNITED
STATES

*Old Cottages, Sulgrave...*

*...still retaining their old-world charm*

At the time of his death, Laurence Washington was living in one of the Spencer houses at Wicken, near the Buckinghamshire border, a gabled house now used as a bakery.

The debt of a great man to his ancestry cannot be estimated; it is impossible to untwine the strands of thought and feeling or to decide where individual endowment begins and ancestral tradition ends.

But there were in the character and thought of George Washington many traits which one can recognise in his Northamptonshire forbears and their families; a particularly keen interest in sheep and wool, the capacity for managing a large estate, the qualities of the soldier, the lawyer, the man of reverend piety, and an almost royal dignity.

*Spring Evening*

# Trail 5
## Great Houghton • Castle Ashby • Yardley Hastings • Easton Maudit

## Great Houghton

THE village sits on the hill close to Northampton overlooking the River Nene. The church is dedicated to St Mary and has an unusual tower with Tuscan columns supporting to the top.

Across the Bedford Road is Little Houghton where the poet John Clare often walked when he was allowed out of the Northampton Asylum (St Andrew's Hospital, Billing Road). (*See Trail 10*). Nearby Clifford Hill was one of his favourite spots, as it has been for Northampton-folk for many years. Surrounded by a deep ditch the hill provides a wide view across one of the fords of the River Nene. It was used by the Romans as a look-out but, according to Arthur Mee, it seems almost certain that it was used much earlier by warring tribes.

*Great Houghton*

*The view from Great Houghton is no longer onto open countryside but to the expanded Northampton*

## Castle Ashby

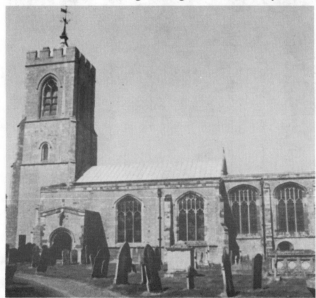

*Church of St Mary, Castle Ashby*

CASTLE ASHBY HOUSE is the country home of the Compton family and dates from 1574, building having been started by the first Lord Compton who was created Earl of Northamptonshire. The gardens are open to the public: the house, which contains many architectural and other treasures, is open occasionally.

Capability Brown fashioned the grounds which extend over a square mile and contain seven ornamental lakes. The private church in the grounds is dedicated to St Mary Magdalene and contains many monuments to the Comptons. There is a fine brass in the chancel floor, dating from 1401, of the rector, William Ermyn. His cope is beautifully decorated with the figures of ten saints standing under canopies.

In the front of the house is a three and a half mile avenue stretching to Yardley Chase which straddles the main Northampton and Bedford road and was once a favourite hunting ground for royalty.

There is a lovely story attached to the house. Sir John Spencer, Lord Mayor of London, had a beautiful daughter, Elizabeth. The first Earl of Northampton, when young, fell in love with her but Sir John sent him packing. Not to be daunted, the Earl devised an ingenious plan to claim his love. One day Sir John happened to pass a baker's boy on the staircase, not knowing that his daughter lay hidden under a cloth in the basket of bread and that the young baker's boy was the Earl! They married against Sir John's will and it took Queen Elizabeth I to smooth things over. When Sir John died the young couple inherited his wealth and became very rich.

George wrote:

Castle Ashby, seat of the Marquess of Northampton, stands boldly on high ground, commanding a far reaching view of the most beautiful parts of the Nene Valley, its lush grasslands, woods and winding streams, with many a spire and tower breaking the distant sky. The village of Castle Ashby has cottages that breathe quiet peace, and gardens which reflect the changing seasons in their wealth of flowers.

*Gateway to the Southern Avenue, Castle Ashby*
*(It remains unchanged today)*

*Castle Ashby*

The gardens at Castle Ashby were originally laid out in the formal style. After the visit of King William III and Queen Mary in 1698 the fourth Earl, in accordance with the King's taste, commenced four great avenues, stretching from the house to the four points of the compass.

Under the seventh and eighth Earls the grounds were completely altered by Capability Brown, three of the avenues disappearing. In the middle of the last century the third Marquess of Northampton formed the terraces and laid out the flower beds broadly as they are today. It was he who brought from Rome the handsome iron-work now seen in the great gates at the head of the southern avenue, which stretches for three miles until it loses itself in the glades of Yardley Chase.

A striking and almost unique feature of Castle Ashby is the series of texts from the Vulgate which form a lettered parapet round the top of the house, and occur in the modern balustrades of the garden terraces: the legend on the east wing runs thus:

*NISI DOMINUS AEDIFICAVERIT DOMUM IN*
*VANUM LABORAVERUNT QUI AEDIFICANT EAM 1624*

*(Except the lord shall have built the house, they will have laboured in vain who are building it 1624. )*

The Sir William Compton who purchased Castle Ashby was so dear to Henry VIII that the king granted him a Royal Augmentation of his arms. To this day the Royal Lion of England looks out from between the three esquire's helmet of the Compton

Arms. It is a fitting reminder of four centuries of devoted service to the person of the Sovereign and to the idea of monarchy. A long line of Comptons has held high office in the Royal Household or served in the Royal Horse Guards.

Two verses from George's poem to Castle Ashby:

*I mourn that change on change must come*
*To many isles of peace,*
*And much of rural charm must pass*
*Before the world's increase,*
*That song of birds and quiet words*
*Amidst earth's discords cease.*

*Yet when the Autumn of the year*
*In fulness nears its close*
*And in the twilight of the West*
*Still beams a blush of rose,*
*Then round earth's sweet suburban ways*
*Steals forth a rich repose.*

## *Yardley Hastings*

THIS village has close links with Castle Ashby and the Marquis of Northampton, for it sits in the middle of the estate. Years ago the then Marquis provided the villagers with a number of first class amenities including a community hall, a reading room and bowling greens.

*Cowper's Oak*

Nearby, in Yardley Chase, was an oak tree called 'Cowper's Oak'. It is said that the poet William Cowper (1731-1800) would walk from his home in Olney through the fields to Yardley Chase and on to the village: it was thought that he sat under the oak in a thunderstorm and wrote the hymn *God moves in a mysterious way*. Alas, the oak is no more, having been burnt down by vandals in 1963. However, we have been able to find an ancient photograph of it in its former glory.

While visiting the village do visit the lovely church of St Andrew with its fine thirteenth century tower. Also in the village is a magnificent former Congregational chapel with four windows and a large pediment, now used for social activities.

*Church of St Andrew, Yardley Hastings*

## Easton Maudit

W E came here on a hot day in July 1991. But let us read George's account of
his visit:

The slender spire of Easton Maudit rises above the wooded country around
Castle Ashby. From 1575 to 1799 the Yelverton family occupied the now vanished
Manor House. They became Earls of Sussex, and occupied high posts in the Royal
Households of the Georgian era.

During this period Northamptonshire held the seats of two ducal families, a
marquis, thirteen earls, two barons and five baronets.

The first Sir Christopher Yelverton, as speaker of the House of Commons in 1597,
wrote the beautiful prayer which is still read at the opening of each day's sessions.
Sir Christopher's prayer stands beside Abraham Lincoln's Gettysburg Address as
one of the supreme expressions of the democratic ideal of government. Its steadfast
reflection of true idealism has so permeated the atmosphere of the House of
Commons, as to make that body the most broadly sympathetic and humane of
legislatures.

Almighty God, by whom alone kings reign and princes decree justice, and from
whom alone cometh all counsel, wisdom and understanding! We thy unworthy
servants, here gathered together in thy name, do most humbly beseech thee
to send down the Heavenly wisdom from above, to direct and guide us all in
our consultations. And grant that, we having thy fear always before our eyes,
and laying aside all private interests, prejudices and partial affections, the result

*Easton Maudit*

of all our counsels may be the glory of thy blessed name, the maintenance of true religion and justice, and the safety, honour and happiness of the king (queen), the public welfare, peace and tranquillity of the realm, and the uniting and knitting together of the hearts of all persons and estates within the same in true Christian love and charity towards one another, through Christ Jesus our Lord and Saviour. Amen.

Sir Christopher and his son, Sir Henry Yelverton, were both great lawyers who became judges. They lie in canopied tombs in the North Chapel of Easton Maudit church, which is also noted for the beautiful tiled floor designed by Lord Alwyne Compton, Bishop of Ely. The tiling contains memorials to three children of Dr Thomas Percy, who was rector here for 29 years from 1765 to 1794, and also held the rectory of Wilby, on the other side of the Nene. From Easton Maudit Dr Percy sent out a steady stream of literary work of great range and variety.

Dr Percy was succeeded by his friend Robert Nares, Keeper of Manuscripts to the British Museum, who while at Easton Maudit helped to complete and prepare for publication the last part of John Bridges' *History of Northamptonshire* issued in 1791.

Dr Percy's house (now the Old Rectory) was visited by Goldsmith, Garrick and Dr Johnson: they are commemorated by a brass in the front pew of the church.

*February Evening*

# Trail 6
## Wollaston • Rushden • Higham Ferrers • Islip • Thorpe Achurch

## Wollaston

*Wollaston Church*

W E searched around the village to find the location of George's sketch and discovered it down a narrow lane next to the church. It is quite unchanged as you can see by our photograph.

*Cottages in Wollaston*

*We were pleased to see that the cottages still retain their thatch*

The church is dedicated to St Mary and is unique in that the tower is in the centre of the church which itself is in the shape of a crucifix.

We quote from George's book on his visit to the village:

Wollaston was once noted for its rush mats, made from rushes gathered by the Nene.

The main part of the church collapsed in the eighteenth century and was rebuilt. Within are wall-tablets to the Dickens family, who lived in the Hall. The church stands high on a hill, and from Beacon Hill is a sweeping view of the Nene country, with twenty-seven towers and spires breaking the skyline.

# Rushden

THE town takes its name from its situation in a 'rushy valley' along the banks of a brook which runs through the town. It was originally a Saxon settlement and by the time of the Norman Conquest was an established village with its own church. A small house on the site of the present Rushden Hall is thought to have been built by John of Gaunt, the Lord of Higham Ferrers Castle, for his park keeper. Rushden Hall was built in the fifteenth century.

Within the last hundred years Rushden has grown from a pastoral village into a small sized town due to the footwear industry, though in the early part of the nineteenth century there were more lacemakers than shoemakers in the town.

The church dedicated to St Mary the Blessed Virgin was formerly a collegiate church. The beautifully proportioned tower is in the Perpendicular style, surmounted by a lofty octagonal crocketed spire rising to a height of 192 feet. Some of the work in the south wall of the chancel dates back to 1250.

There are tombs to the Pemberton family: Sir Godfrey lies in his armour and another tomb has the figures of Sir Robert and his wife, with their four sons and four daughters. Sir Robert was a Gentleman Usher to Elizabeth I.

George Harrison wrote a fine poem to the village: here are the first two verses:

*A blending of the new world and the old,*
*In Rushden greets the stranger passing by,*
*Save when the hues of early morn enfold*
*The lowland meadows and the tranquil sky,*
*Or in that magic hour when coming night*
*Mellows the sun's last beams of fading light.*

*Old cottages, moss grown with age and time,*
*Stand shaded still by gnarled and ancient trees,*
*That oft-times waken to their wonted rhyme*
*When Spring comes smiling on the southern breeze,*
*To leave the twinkling leaf buds strangely fair,*
*Soft points of crimson in the dancing air.*

*The Spire of St Mary's Church, Rushden*

# Higham Ferrers

LIKE Rushden, Higham Ferrers has expanded with the development of the footwear industry. Have a look around the vicinity of the church for some really old buildings. The High Street contains many houses of local limestone with Collyweston tiles (*see the first volume of 'Wanderers in Northamptonshire' for some information about these*).

St Mary's is a large and ambitious church, with a large elegant crocketed spire with flying butresses to support it, and is as old as the Magna Carta. It contains many treasures and is well worth a visit. There are a number of interesting brasses including several to the Chichele family, though, surprisingly, not one to Henry Chichele who was Archbishop of Canterbury from 1414 until he died in 1443. The frontal on the High Altar is made from locally tanned leather and was presented to the church by a local shoe factory, John White, in 1970.

Archbishop Chichele's Bede House was founded in 1428 as a hospital – this is the building to the south of the church. The building to the north west of the church is the school which was founded in 1422.

The Market Place close to the church along the main A6 road is very old and is well worth visiting. From Whellan's *History, Gazetteer and Directory of Northamptonshire, 1849* we quote:

> *There was once a castle to the north of the church: the date of its erection cannot be ascertained, but it is supposed to have been built by one of the family of Ferrers.*

*West Doorway, Church of the Blessed Virgin Mary, Higham Ferrers*

*The situation it occupied is plainly indicated by earthworks, from which an idea of its great strength and extent may be conceived.*

A quotation from 1540: *The castel, now of late faullen and taken doune.* So the castle disappeared a long time ago.

Another quote from Whellan's *History* concerns Henry Chichele:

*He was born of an obscure family in this town in 1360. Tradition tells that when a boy, keeping his father's sheep near Higham, he was noticed by William of Wykeham, who was so pleased with the talent displayed in his answers that he took him under his patronage, and promoted him in his college.*

George wrote:

Upon entering Higham Ferrers from whatever direction, one is instantly impressed by its beautiful church spire, which dominates the whole town. A few weeks

*Around the West Door there are elaborate carvings depicting scenes from the life of Christ*

ago I saw it etched against a sky of delicate blue. The sun, low in the west, shone upon it to make clear-cut each delicate ornament and line, and I marvelled at its wonderful symmetry.

How ably these early builders arranged their masses of light, breaking them with just sufficient shadow to give added dignity and repose to the whole building. The spire rises to 170 feet, the tower contains a clock and eight bells: the spire fell early in the 17th century and was rebuilt in 1632 strictly on the lines of the original structure. The church was restored in 1864. A new organ was installed in 1930 to replace the one built in 1877.

My thoughts go back to the time when I first knew this ancient borough, more than half a century ago. It seemed to me then like one of those quaint country towns which one associates with Worcestershire and Gloucestershire. Even as I visit now, the similarity is pronounced, for the principal street retains much of its former character.

## *Islip*

A CLOSE neighbour of Thrapston, just across the bridge, we find here the church of St Nicholas which dates from the fifteenth century.

*The Church of St Nicholas, Islip*

More American influence can be discovered. In the church, in the south wall of the sanctuary, is a monument to Mary Washington whose, uncle, John, was uncle to Laurence Washington who was great grandfather of George Washington.

*The Spring flowers were coming into bloom when we*
*visited the church*

The view that George drew has hardly changed, as you can see. He wrote:

Also in the church is a modern brass tablet replacing a missing brass of 1467, to John Nicoll and Annys his wife. This brass, the beautiful oak screen, stalls and reredos are from the designs of Mr Temple Moore, and were dedicated on 13st August 1911. A brass tablet on the screen is inscribed:

THIS SCREEN TOGETHER WITH THE STALLS AND REREDOS, WERE ERECTED BY DE LANCY NICOLL AND BENJAMIN NICOLL, OF N. YORK, IN 1911, TO COMMEMORATE THEIR ANCESTOR MATTHIAS NICOLL, WHO WAS SECRETARY OF THE DUKE OF YORK'S EXPEDI- TION, DEPARTED TO AMERICA 1664, AND AFTER THE CAPTURE OF NEW AMSTERDAM BECAME MAYOR OF NEW YORK 1671, SPEAKER OF THE FIRST COLONIAL ASSEMBLY WRITER OF THE DUKES LAWS, AND DIED 22nd DECEMBER, 1687, AND WAS BURIED AT MANCHASSET, LONG ISLAND U. S. A.

## *Thorpe Achurch*

A LTHOUGH George's sketch is of Thorpe Achurch you will not, today, find this village named on the map. After some research we discovered that it is now two villages: Thorpe Waterville and Achurch. To quote from Whellan's *History* of 1849:

*The village of Achurch, which is small, is four and a half miles from N.NE. of Thrapston. Thorpe, or Thorpe Waterville, is a small hamlet in this parish. Though no distinct mention is made in Domesday-book of Thorpe Manor, yet it appears in early records to have been the capital manor. The addition of Waterville has been taken from its early possessors. Here was formerly a castle, probably built by Azelin de Waterville. John de Achurch, a monk of Peterborough Abbey, compiled the register respecting the affairs of that convent, from himself, named Achurch, which is still extant, and in the library of the Dean and Chapter of that cathedral.*

There are four hamlets, all connected, around the district. Achurch and Lilford were Saxon settlements and Thorpe Waterville, along with Wigsthorpe, was Danish. The church that serves them all is at Achurch, built in the shape of a cross by Sir Asceline de Waterville as a thanks for a safe return from the Crusades.

The Revd Robert Browne, for forty years Rector of Thorpe Achurch and known as the Father of Congregationalism, made a great indirect contribution to the American Constitution. He was the first to proclaim the Congregation Order of Church Government, and to claim that the Christian Church was separate from the State. One direct result of this doctrine was the sailing of the Pilgrim Fathers to Massachusetts in 1620. The American Republic has always maintained complete separation of Church and State. Browne was of

*Cottage, Thorpe Achurch, in which Robert Browne,*
*the Father of Congregationalism, preached.*

*The fire which seriously damaged Robert Browne's cottage*

Kettering Evening Telegraph

*… happily now restored*

Rutlandshire birth and a kinsman of Lord Burleigh. Even as Rector he frequently held services outside the Church. He suffered many imprisonments and died in Northampton gaol. His grave is in St Giles' churchyard, Northampton.

Robert Browne's cottage, Chapel Cottage, is in Thorpe Waterville and was devastated by fire in 1979 but is now tastefully restored. It has a wonderful inglenook fireplace and a priest's hole.

*(Our grateful thanks to the residents of Chapel Cottage for their help, and also to the 'Kettering Evening Telegraph' for permission to print the photograph of the fire.)*

A memorial to Robert Browne was erected in 1923. The plaque on it reads:

TO THE MEMORY OF ROBERT BROWNE,
A FOUNDER OF THE BROWNISTS, OR
INDEPENDENTS. RECTOR OF THORPE
ACHURCH, 1591 – 1631 WHO WAS BURIED
IN THE CHURCHYARD
8TH OCT. 1633.
A TRIBUTE TO A LIFE WHEREIN, AMONG
MANY THINGS OBSCURE, ONE THING
SHONE BRIGHTLY, THAT CHRIST WAS BY
HIM EXALTED AS HEAD ABOVE ALL.
ERECTED BY CONGREGATIONALISTS IN
CONNECTION WITH THE VISIT TO
NORTHAMPTON, OCT 1923, OF THE
CONGREGATIONAL UNION OF ENGLAND
AND WALES.

*Gathering in the Hay Harvest*

# Trail 7
## Titchmarsh • Thrapston • Denford • Woodford

## Titchmarsh

*Set high upon a breezy hill,*
*With woods and meadows far below,*
*The streets look down upon the mill*
*And little paths that winding go*
*By corn fields where the poppies burn,*
*To roll away with a curve and sweep,*
*Till lost in nodding ling and fern,*
*And woodland shadows lush and deep.*

*The church, half hid by speading trees*
*(St Mary's, Titchmarsh)*

TITCHMARSH is one of our favourite Northamptonshire villages, and nothing much seems to have changed since George's visit. Both the Pickering and Dryden families lived here and the Church of St Mary contains several memorials to them. In the church also is a marvellous collection of Victorian wall paintings by Mrs Agnes Saunders and Miss Anson.

The church architecture is unique with what is claimed to be the finest parish church tower anywhere in the country outside Somerset. It soars to the height of 99 ft. and during the reign of Queen Elizabeth I a beacon was installed at the top of the tower to warn of the Spanish Armada.

It is the only church to be surrounded by a ha-ha (a sunken fence which keeps cattle out without obstructing the view).

The beautiful statues in the niches on the tower are fairly modern and are said to have been paid for by the rector's wife in 1901 from the sale of her fantail pigeons.

This is what George wrote:

Titchmarsh was the home of John Dryden's parents, and here he spent his boyhood. His mother's uncle, Sir Gilbert Pickering, Bt. , owned the Manor House, and little John probably sat with him in the cosy family pew with its fireplace, set above the porch of the church, whose glorious tower soars for ninety-nine feet above the hill. John's cousin, Betty Pickering (Mrs John Creed ) mother of Mrs Stewart of Cotterstock, was living at the Manor House, and after Dryden's decease in 1700 she placed this endearing epitaph to him in Titchmarsh church, where his parents, Erasmus and Mary Dryden, lie buried;

JOHN DRYDEN, ESQ. ,
THE CELEBRATED POET AND LAUREATE OF HIS TIME.
HIS BRIGHT PARTS AND LEARNING ARE BEST SEEN IN HIS
OWN EXCELLENT WRITINGS ON VARIOUS SUBJECTS.
WE BOAST, THAT HE WAS BRED AND HAD
HIS FIRST LEARNING HERE;
WHERE HE HAS OFTEN MADE US HAPPIE
BY HIS KIND VISITS AND DELIGHTFUL CONVERSATION.
HE MARRIED THE LADY ELIZABETH HOWARD, DAUGHTER TO
HENRY(*) EARL OF BERKSHIRE; BY WHOM HE HAD THREE
SONS, CHARLES JOHN AND ERASMUS-HENRY;
AND, AFTER 70 ODD YEARES, WHEN NATURE COULD BE NO
LONGER SUPPORTED, HE RECEIVED THE NOTICE OF
HIS APPROACHING DISSOLUTION
WITH SWEET SUBMISSION AND ENTIRE RESIGNATION
TO THE DIVINE WILL;
AND HE TOOK SO TENDER AND OBLIGING A FAREWELL OF
HIS FRIENDS, AS NONE BUT HIMSELF COULD HAVE
EXPRESSED; OF WHICH SORROWFUL NUMBER
I WAS ONE.
HIS BODY WAS HONOURABLY INTERRED IN WESTMINSTER
ABBY, AMONG THE GREATEST WITS OF DIVERS AGES

* This is a mistake. She was the daughter of Thomas, first Earl, who died in 1669.

*Our view of George's scene. St Mary's, Titchmarsh*

# Thrapston

*An old-world atmosphere round Thrapston clings*
*In quiet peace of long remembered things.*

EORGE'S sketch of the lovely seventeenth century bridge over the Nene is now overshadowed by the concrete monstrosity of the A1-M1 link road across the Nene meadows between Thrapston and Denford. However, there is

one consolation – it has taken a great deal of traffic away from the town and
made it as peaceful as George remembered it.

*Bridge over the Nene at Thrapston*

*...unchanged today, but for the traffic lights!*

Here in Thrapston and nearby Islip are yet more American connections. In the Thrapston churchyard lies Sir John Washington, brother of Laurence Washington whose son emigrated to America and became the great-grandfather of the president, while Sir John's wife lies in Islip church. Montagu House was thought to be the home of Sir John.

George wrote:

Above Titchmarsh we enter one of the lovliest reaches of the Nene – that between Islip and Thrapston. The ground rises steeply from each side of the river, and here, for the first time, we see signs of modern industry – the great blast furnaces on the hill above Islip, and the large foundry at Thrapston. (*Perhaps the older readers can remember where these were. J & VW.* ) It was only a glimpse, and we are soon again in rural peace until we reach Irthlingborough.

## *Denford*

*Dear Denford lies in twinkling haze*
*Above the rivers widening brim;*
*By deep'ning woods' entangled maze*
*And rose wreath'd gardens fair and trim.*
*Beyond the trees the uplands rise*
*In varied colours, fold on fold,*
*That catch the glory of the skies,*
*The flush of morn's and evening's gold.*

W^E keep returning to this delightful village which, now that it has a by-pass, is once more peaceful as George would have known it.

*Our view of the Church of Holy Trinity, Denford...*

The spire of the lovely church of the Holy Trinity adorns the skyline. If you look on the wall above the choir stalls you will see some vases let into the wall. These were used in earlier times as a type of loudspeaker – when the rector was preaching the vases gave the voice an added resonance so that people at the back could hear.

Parking is restricted in the village so please park carefully to avoid annoying not only the human residents but also our fine feathered friends that live on the river.

George wrote:

Beyond Denford, we soon come to Woodford Mill, a favourite spot for boating parties, and land to see the famous wooden effigies in the St Mary the Virgin church – two of the few remaining medieval painted figures. They commemorate Sir Walter

*...and as George saw it*

Trailly (d. 1290) and his wife Eleanor (d. 1580) and a tablet to John Cole, County Historian, schoolmaster and naturalist (1792-1848).

# Woodford

*The river lined by willow trees*
*Flows smoothly on its level way,*
*Or kissed to eddies by the breeze*
*Which sparkle in the light of day.*
*Deep through the long, cool meadow grass*
*The browsing cattle idly wade,*
*And at the noontide slowly pass*
*To seek the aspen's welcome shade.*

*Woodford Mill*

*Now seated here beyond the mill,*
*I see the changing colours flow;*
*The shadows in the water spill*
*From little clouds, that drifting go*
*Across the tender sky of blue,*
*To mirror in the river's tide,*
*Like little boats of magic hue*
*That only fairies deign to guide.*

*The site of Woodford Mill – alas! no more*

WOODFORD, a large but still beautiful village, is well worth exploring, especially down by the church. You can take an attractive riverside walk along the Nene Way to the site of an old mill although, alas!, the mill is no more.

The church of St Mary the Virgin stands proud by the side of the Nene. This is worth a visit to see the tomb of Sir Walter Trailly, who died in 1290, surmounted not by a stone effigy but by one of only a few wooden figures. His wife, Alianora lays at his side. In a pillar in a glass case, wrapped in a cloth, is

*Wooden effigies in Woodford Church*

a human heart. This could be one of the Trailly family who died in the Crusades, for it was a practice in those days to inter the heart at the home of the deceased.

We visited this lovely place again on a sunny afternoon in July 1992 and, walking down the lane near the church, witnessed an amazing scene at the farm at the bottom. The lady of the farm, Mrs Prentiss, was feeding her animals – a marvellous sight, with ducks, geese, sheep, hens, guinea fowl and a wonderful collection of goats. She is doing a fine job of reviving old and nearly extinct breeds of both sheep and goats.

*May Woods*

# Trail 8
Orlingbury • Walgrave • Mears Ashby • Wilby • Ecton

## *Orlingbury*

WE called here during the summer of 1991, dodging heavy showers and thunderstorms – which were well needed as we were in the second year of below average rainfall. The village has many very good buildings to look at, especially around the green.

Orlingbury was the home of one Jack Batsaddle who resided at Batsaddle Lodge, by Batsaddle Woods. The lodge is, sadly, no more, having been demolished a few years ago. According to legend Jack slew the last wolf in England. His tomb in the Church of St Mary is very imposing, an effigy of a man in armour. He was reputed to have died from drinking very cold water after his battle with the wolf.

*Recumbent, carved in heavy stone,*
*Batsaddle in the old church lies,*
*He fought the wolf, the last, alone,*
*Beneath the burning Summer skies,*
*Heated and sore, he stooped to drink*
*From stream that winds through meadows wide,*
*Then sank beside the flowering brink*
*And weary with exhaustion died.*

*Old Green, Orlingbury*

*Church of St Mary, the Blessed Virgin, Orlingbury*

Again we have a church dedicated to St Mary the Blessed Virgin and of the Perpendicular period. It has an imposing tower with filigree battlements and very tall pinnacles.

We like George's description of his visit:

Orlingbury, in the early days of my first acquaintance, always appeared to me as a drowsy village. I have sat here for hours under the shadows of the ancient elm trees, with nothing to disturb my musings but the milk cows coming from or going to the fields, or the old carrier's cart jog-trotting to Wellingborough or Kettering on market days. Occasionally an old lady with poke bonnet would come to the well on the green (in those days worked with a winding chain) to fill buckets with water, or toddling infants gather dandelions or daisies from the grass. In the autumn of the year, and during hay harvest, the lumbering waggons would pass and repass to the farms, giving that ideal rural atmosphere beloved by the town dweller.

## Walgrave

WE visited Walgrave one Sunday when they were raising funds for the church of St Peter. The church had also been extensively restored in 1868 at a cost of £1, 500. The spire was partially taken down and rebuilt, the walls were cleaned of unsightly plaster and repointed, new high pitched roofs were replaced and open oak replaced the old pews.

John Williams who was rector here became Archbishop of York in the reign of Charles I.

## Mears Ashby

OUR visit to this village, steeped in history and folklore, was on a cold and frosty morning in January 1991 when we learned the story of the 'Tinker's

*The Church of St Peter, Walgrave*

Tree'. One day, many many years ago, a tinker called, selling his wares and mending pots. He sat on the green, spread his wares on the grass and, after a few drinks, dozed off. Just before he went to sleep he stuck his walking stick in the ground and when he awoke it had taken root and it grew into a fine study elm. Near the spot where he sat is a house called 'The Tinker's Tree' and also close by is a road called 'Tinker's Crescent'. We heard a whisper that there used to be an inn by the same name but that is now no more.

The second story we heard was of one Sarah Bradshaw. She was branded as a witch and, to prove whether she was innocent or guilty, was ducked in the Manor pond – for in those days it was believed that suspected witches, if innocent, would sink and, if guilty, would rise to the surface for sentence. She sank, and it is said that on some dark nights she can be seen haunting the pond!

*The Church of All Saints, Mears Ashby*

*...and our view*

# Wilby

THE church, dedicated to St Mary, sits at the top of Church Lane. It is one of the few churches in Northamptonshire to have flying buttresses supporting the spire. Inside the church is a fine Jacobean pulpit.

William the Conquerer gave his niece Judith this village with four hides of land (a hide was a somewhat variable area of land, sufficient to provide the needs of one household).

A story we were told was of the Wilby witch named Kate. She had a husband named Tom, a woodsman. One day, while at work in the forest, Tom sat down to eat his food but found that it had been stolen. He could see no one about except his black cat so next day he lay in wait to catch the thief. Lo and behold, the cat came and took the food. Tom jumped up quickly with his axe and as quick as a flash cut off the cat's paw. But when Tom got home that night he found his wife with one of her hands missing – chopped of at the wrist!

*St Mary's Church, Wilby, as George saw it in 1937*

*Wilby church today*

## Ecton

*Ecton Church, Evening*

*The blush of evening on an old church tower,*
*That smooths the rugged stones to tender grace,*
*And gives a touch of magic to an hour*
*Where lines of gold and shadow interlace*
*With gentleness, until the colours blend*
*In changing hues that seem to have no end.*

AGAIN the American influence predominates for it was here that the Franklins lived for over three hundred years, the forebears of Benjamin Franklin. He was known as the 'Father of the American Constitution', having helped to frame the constitution, and had been active in promoting the Declaration of Independence in 1733. He was also a notable scientist who invented the lightning conductor.

The Franklins were the village blacksmiths and their smithy is thought to have been in the High Street where the Three Horseshoes Inn now stands.

*Church of St Mary, Ecton*

Thomas and Eleanor, uncle and aunt of Benjamin Franklin, are buried in the churchyard to the left of the church door, just before you enter the church porch. The tree close by was planted by the Americans in their memory.

Another local inn is the World's End Inn. There are two theories of the origin of this name. One relates it to the Royalist's retreat from the Battle of Naseby when, so it is said, some of the defeated soldiers took refuge in the cellar of the inn. The alternative explanation (which we favour) is that the artist Hogarth visited Ecton Rectory on several occasions, once when he was working on his famous painting *The End of the World*. He used to visit the inn and on one occasion he offered to paint an inn sign for the innkeeper based on this work. The innkeeper readily agreed and changed the name of the inn to 'The World's End'. The sign was erected on the other side of the road but, sadly, was stolen within a few months, never to be seen again.

The church of St Mary was built of ironstone in the late thirteenth century. The Franklins were Protestants during the reign of Mary Tudor and they hid the family bible inside a stool. During bible readings someone always stood by the door as a look out – for they could have been imprisoned if they had been caught.

The village has held on to its own individuality during a period of expansion, the Manor House having been tastefully restored into luxurious apartments. We think that George would have liked the work carried out.

Here are his notes on Ecton:

Josiah Franklin and his wife of Ecton left for Boston Massachusetts about 1684. Josiah's youngest son, Benjamin, was born in 1702 of a second marriage. That the United States survived the War of Independence of 1776 – 1783 was due to the fact that the character of George Washington held the little, ill clad, ill paid army together until the tact and ability of Benjamin Franklin secured the aid of France. Franklin has been called 'the first American' – the first man, who by his own merit rose from the humblest to the highest station. When in England as plenipotentiary of the colonists, before the Revolution, Franklin visited Ecton and traced his own ancestry back to 1555. The Franklins had long held thirty acres freehold and a forge, which latter stood where the Three Horseshoes Inn now stands.

The Franklins were able and upright. In the year 1910 American admirers of Franklin presented to the church a bronze plaque with a portrait in relief and this inscription, which closes with a quotation all the more notable, that Benjamin Franklin had, in earlier years, been a marked free thinker;

BENJAMIN FRANKLIN.
BORN JAN. 7th. 1706. DIED APRIL 17, 1790
HIS ANCESTORS WERE BORN IN THIS
VILLAGE AND MANY OF HIS RELATIVES
ARE BURIED IN THIS CHURCHYARD

"I HAVE LIVED FOR A LONG TIME
81 YEARS AND THE LONGER I
LIVE THE MORE CONVINCING PROOF
I SEE OF THIS TRUTH THAT GOD
GOVERNS IN THE AFFAIRS OF MEN"

These words, with the possible exception of '81 years' were spoken in late June, 1787, before the constitutional convention, at a critical moment in the discussion leading to the formation of the American Constitution. A complete deadlock had been reached on the question of proportional representation of the states in the federal government. Franklin rose, uttered the above words and solemnly proposed 'imploring the assitance of heaven'. He advocated the opening of the morning sessions with prayer. Shortly afterwards a harmonious solution to the problem was discovered.

The Englishmen who emigrated to America took with them a conception of civil law and civil rights based ultimately on the Magna Carta.

At Easter 1215, the Barons gathered at Brackley, the southern most borough of Northamptonshire, and thence forwarded their claim to the Charter to the King at Oxford. "Why do they not ask for my kingdom ?" cried John; but the Barons had actually won the day. From Brackley they marched on London, which opened its gates to them, and the submission at Runnymede followed swiftly. Among the Barons who drew up the Magna Carta were two ancestors of George Washington, first President of the United States of America.

# Trail 9

### Brixworth• East Haddon• Pitsford• Lamport•
### Great Brington• Little Brington

## Brixworth

WE know this village well, and visit it quite often, for our family lives here. This is what George had to say:

*The Church of All Saints, Brixworth*

The Church of All Saints, Brixworth, stands on high ground to the north of the village, an austere pile which has looked down upon thirteen centuries of history. It was built in basilica form by monks from Medehamstede (Peterborough) about AD680, and is thus the second oldest church in England, the oldest being St Martin's, Canterbury. With the rubble stone the builders skilfully combined red Roman tiles, notably in the arches of the nave. The church was ravaged by the Danes, and restored in a somewhat different form, first by the Saxon and later by mediaeval builders. It was further restored and greatly altered in 1864-6. Towards the end of the Saxon period the side aisles were removed, and the arches of the nave filled in, so that their red tile mouldings are now visible both from without and within. All Saints, Brixworth, is a most impressive sight. It has justly been called 'the most instructive monument in the early history of our national architecture.'

The village contains some fine seventeenth and eighteenth century houses.

Brixworth has long been a centre for hunting and is the home of the Pytchley hunt, the neo-Georgian kennels and stables being close to the village.

## East Haddon

HERE the village pump sits under a thatched roof. The church of St Mary is Norman. The hall close by was built in 1780-1 for the Sawbridge family by John Wagstaff of Daventry.

It was an old custom that villagers took their Sunday joints to the baker who would cook them in his oven. In East Haddon they would ring a bell in the church when the roasts were ready – this was known as the 'pudding bell'.

Reading from Whellan's *Directory* of 1849 we learn that:

*The gravel pits adjoining the road to Ravensthorpe furnish fibrous gypsom, jasper and stone marl, and of extreneous fossils, gryphites, ammonites, belemites, escallop shells, muscles, and corallites. A quantity of human bones were discovered imbedded in gravel about 15 years since in a field a little north of the village belonging to the Rev. W. Smyth.*

*There is a strong chalybeate spring in Mr. Sawbridge's garden.*

*The old thatched pump in East Haddon*

# Pitsford

THIS delightful village stands at the head of Pitsford reservoir, the water supply for Northampton town, opened by the Queen Mother in 1956. The site was chosen because of the prolific springs in the area, numbering over three hundred.

The church of All Saints was restored in 1866. It has a lovely Norman door, and the tower dates from the thirteenth century.

On browsing through an old local history book we learned that the quarry on the Harborough Road once provided a very hard stone that was used for ovens and fire hearths. Also, we discovered that the cottage close by, in the dip of the Harborough Road by the reservoir, was probably the old toll house or was built on the site of this.

We found George's cottages (*page 80*) changed slightly since his day (*our picture is on page 81*). However, they have been tastefully restored and are still in their thatch. We think George would have been pleased with the result. Close by the cottages is the old forge, now closed.

*Old Cottages, Pitsford*

# Lamport

THE Church of All Saints sits across the road from Lamport Hall, the ancestral home of the Ishams from 1560-1976, and now maintained by the Lamport Hall Trust. For a while it was the home of the Northampton Record Society. The Trust is very active and numerous craft fairs and other activities are held throughout the year.

We were reminded of a sad story when we stopped to photograph the swans on the entrance to the hall on the A508 Northampton/Market Harborough road.

During a party at Brixworth Hall one of the guests thought that he would have a joke on Sir Justinian Isham – who was an abstemious man – by painting the swans red. He climbed up on the gate pier but missed his footing and fell, clasping one of the birds. The beak of the swan, being made of cast iron, pierced his chest. He was rushed to a doctor in Market Harborough but there he died.

*The old cottages in Pitsford today*

*Church of All Saints, Lamport*

*George's view of Lamport Church*

Looking through the archives we discovered that a namesake of ours, Edward Worlidge, worked at the Hall in 1671 and received a wage of £8 per annum including board and lodgings.

The staffing at Lamport Hall in the early 1850s was as follows: 'twelve resident servants consisting of: a butler, a footman and a gardener on the male side; a cook/housekeeper, two ladies maids, two house maids, a laundry maid, a dairy maid, a kitchen maid and a nursemaid on the female side'.

Their annual wages were: cook/housekeeper £18, dairy and kitchen maids £9, butler £47, footman £17, coachman £52.

*One of the Lamport swans*

## Great Brington

THIS village is on the estates of Althorp House, the home of the Spencer family who have lived here for over 400 years. The most famous Spencer is, of course, Lady Diana Spencer (Princess Diana) who married Prince Charles. In the lovely church of St Mary is the beautiful and sumptious private Spencer Chapel.

Also in the church is the tomb of Laurence Washington, an ancestor of George Washington, although we have to go down to Little Brington to see where they lived.

*Tomb of Sir John and Dame Isabella Spencer, 1522*

There is yet another connection between Great Brington Church and the history of America. The church tower was chosen to hold the southern-most of the Northamptonshire beacons whose flames heralded the approach of the Spanish Armada in 1588. Hence the news was flashed to Rockingham in the

*The Cross, Great Brington Green*
*(Probably marking the spot where Christianity was first preached in the district)*

north-west, and through Ecton and Titchmarsh to Ufford in the Soke of Peterborough. The course of the next six days battle in the English Channel decided the future history of America, the purpose of Spain being to crush a possible rival to her American Empire and to secure the ports, ship-building yards and forests of England for her own transatlantic shipping.

*The Arms of Lawrence Washington, 1588, impaled with those of Butler*

George's notes:

The church of St Mary the Virgin, Great Brington, a few miles north-west of Northampton, stands on a high ridge overlooking a valley to the north. From it one looks across the great park of Althorp, with its noble avenues leading from the mansion to Great and Little Brington. Since the days of Henry VII, Althorp has belonged to the Spencers, and after the burning of their earlier home at Wormleighton by Prince Rupert

*The original window, with these Arms, is preserved at Weston Hall, Towcester, and a copy has been set in its place at Sulgrave Manor.*

on the night before the battle of Edgehill, Althorp has been their main family seat. The present chancel, clerestory and north chapel were built by Sir John Spencer about the year 1514, and in this beautifully lighted chapel are gathered the memorials of the Spencer family, which constitute one of the finest collections of coloured sculpture and heraldic emblems in England. The fineness of the sculpture, the delicacy of the colouring and the richness of the heraldry make a visit to the Spencer Chapel a notable experience for the art-lover, and the student of social history. (*A very private place JW.*)

In the nave and choir of Great Brington Church are two simpler memorials which yet have great historic interest. In the nave is a brass to Robert Washington and his wife Elizabeth, who both died in March 1622. On the brass are the arms of the Sulgrave branch of the Washington family, two red bars across a silver (white) shield, between them a crescent, above three five-pointed red spur-rowels. The crescent denotes that the Sulgrave Washingtons were a junior branch of the Washingtons of Warton, Lancashire. In the choir is a tombstone carved with the arms of Laurence Washington, impaled with the Butler arms of his wife's family. In Laurence's arms there is no crescent, for in 1592 he received from Clarenceux, Kings of Arms, a

*Church of St Mary, Great Brington*

grant establishing his right to omit this. The Arms of his descendents, including the Washingtons of Virginia, have therefore, no crescent.

The Washingtons were cousins of the Spencers, and at the time of financial difficulty were given a home at Brington. Robert resided there for over twenty years; he held a family pew and benches for his servants;he was a trustee of the Brington Charity, and farmed sixty acres of land adjoining the Spencer land. He is always spoken of as 'Robert Washington of Great Brington, Gentleman'. He was on friendliest terms with the Spencers; and in 1599 Sir John Spencer left his wife a legacy in thanks for her care of him in his last illness.

The cousinship between the Spencers and the Washingtons is traceable to a common descent, on the distaff side, from the Kytsons of Warton Hall, Lancashire.

As Laurence Washington was the direct ancestor of George Washington, first President of the United States, it is worth while to give in full the inscription on his tomb.

HERE LIETH THE BODI OF LAVRENCE
WASHINGTON SONNE AND HEIRE OF
ROBERT WASHINGTON OF SOVLGRAVE
IN THE COVNTIE OF NORTHAMTON
ESQVIER WHO MARRIED MARGARET
THE ELDEST DAVGHTER OF WILLIAM
BVTLER OF TEES IN THE COVNTIE
OF SVSSEXE WHO HAD ISSV
BY HER 8 SONNS & 9 DAVGHTERS
WHICH LAVRENCE DECESSED THE 13
OF DECEMBER A. DNI 1616

THOV THAT BY CHANCE OR CHOYCE
OF THIS HAST SIGHT
KNOW LIFE TO DEATH RESIGNES
AS DAYE TO NIGHT
BUT AS THE SVNNS RETORNE
REVIVES THE DAYE
SO CHRIST SHALL VS
THOVGH TVRNDE TO DVST & CLAY

## Little Brington

WE came down the road from Great Brington in search of the home of the Washingtons. Originally living at Sulgrave Manor, their reduced financial circumstances forced them to move to Little Brington where the then Lord Spencer found them a simple residence which became known as 'Washington Cottage'. George drew it but, sadly, the original cottage is no more, having been burnt down in 1960. We met a gentleman just leaving his allotment who told us that the road by the cottage was being repaired one day and when the road-menders went to lunch they left their steam-roller puffing away and a spark from the funnel ignited the thatch.

The site of Washington Cottage is now occupied by a house designed by our friend Mr J T Neville who drew the architectural sketches in the first volume

*Little Brington, The Green*
*(The 'Washington House' has four chimney stacks.)*

*The scene today. All that remains is the tree!*

of *Wanderers*. All that is left of the original cottage is the plaque from the wall, but if you look carefully you can see that some of the original stone has been used to build the centre part of the new house.

The plaque reads:

THE LORD GEVETH
THE LORD TAKETH
AWAY BLESSED BE THE
NAME OF THE LORD
CONSTRVCTA
1606

*Winter Sunset*

# Trail 10
The Soke of Peterborough • Peterborough • Helpstone

## The Soke of Peterborough

ALTHOUGH it was originally in Northamptonshire, boundary changes have resulted in the Soke being 'poached' by Cambridgeshire. However George had much to write about it, and the area has so many links with Northamptonshire that we have included it in this collection.

Here is George's introduction:

This part of Northamptonshire seems to slip naturally into the flat fen country of Lincolnshire, which adjoins on the north and west.

The Liberty or Soke of Peterborough is a separate administrative county, distinct from the remainder of Northamptonshire.

Stamford Baron is that lesser portion of the municipal borough of Stamford. The Great North Road runs along the picturesque High Street of Stamford Baron (*it now by-passes the town JW*) and the Inn was a famous posting house, in whose lobbies travellers waited for coaches going north and south. The old sign still hangs above the street, near the Welland bridge on the Lincolnshire side of which rises the spire of St Mary's church. From the High Street one reaches the entrance lodges to Burghley Park, soon after entering which the visitor gets a glimpse of Burghley House on a slight rise to the right. Burghley House is a superb example of

*Burghley House from the distance*

*The George, Stamford Baron and St Mary's, Stamford*

Elizabethan architecture. It is built of Barnack Rag, which has mellowed but not worn. Part of the house lies in Barnack parish. The Romans discovered fine stone at Barnack: in the Middle Ages Barnack Rag was used to build the cathedrals at Peterborough, Ely and Bury St Edmunds, also Ramsey Abbey, and many fine churches in Northamptonshire and East Anglia. Barnack church is of Saxon origin, though Norman and later English is also found here.

The lovely town of Stamford has recently become known to TV viewers for it was the location for much of BBC2's production of George Eliot's *Middlemarch.* You will find another of George's sketches of the town on page 96.

## Peterborough

GEORGE writes: Peterborough is an ancient city and seat of a diocese, a municipal borough, and polling place for the Peterborough division of the county. It is situated on the north bank of the Nene.

The history of the Cathedral Church of St Peter, from which the city derives its name, is of great interest, and dates back to very early times. It was the conventual church of one of the wealthiest Benedictine abbeys in England. It was founded, according to the Saxon Chronicle, in the year AD655 by Peada, son of Penda, King of Mercia, and perhaps with the exception of Lichfield, was the first resting place of Christianity in central England.

My own personal impression of Peterborough Cathedral is always one of awed reverence, although I have never wholly recovered from my first visit, which was

*An Autumn Day, Peterborough*

*Entrance to Deanery, Peterborough Cathedral*

one of disappointment with the interior. It seemed to me then, as it still does, to lack the dignity which I expected to continue the glories of the West Front, which is a pearl of the purest character.

It wil be noticed that the West Front consists of three majestic arches 81 feet in height; these are supported by triangular-shafted piers. This magnificent structure, seen under favourable lighting, is impressive, one of earth's loveliest possessions, inspired by the loftiest ambitions of man.

One other ancient building should be mentioned, namely the Market Cross, or Old Town Hall, in the Market Place(*now in the pedestrian precinct. JW*). The building, which is of stone, was reconstructed in 1671;the upper portion, which rests on a arcade of round arches, was at various times, used by the Magistrates as a court-room and by the Corporation for their official business until the new Town Hall was built. The open space below was formerly used as a butter and poultry market.

Much more could be written of the beauties of Peterborough and its ancient history, but we would need a very large volume to collate all that was needed to do the city justice. However, a visit to the Tourist Information Office (45 Bridge Street) will enable you to obtain plenty of material that will help you to make an enjoyable and instructive tour of the city.

# *Helpstone*

THIS village also has become part of Cambridgeshire although at the time of George's visit it was in the Soke of Peterborough. However, we felt that it must be included here as it has a very close connection to Northamptonshire through the poet John Clare who was born on the 13th July 1793.

To most people Helpstone is known by its associations with John Clare, who was born here on the 13th July, 1793, in a small cottage degraded by popular tradition to a mud hut. I was a boy of not more than seven or eight years when I read a life of John Clare, and to this day I remember what a profound influence that book had upon me. I read and re-read portions of it for many months, the poems I soon learned to know by heart, and the simple unaffected style may have had some influence on my own small efforts later in life. The fact that the youthful John Clare started off one morning to reach the place where the sky joined the earth, seemed to me so perfectly the natural thing for a child imbued with poetic fancies to do, that I was simply charmed by the idea. The cottage, too, though pictured as a very humble place, seemed a most romantic place to me and a most desirable one for a future poet to be born in. I was not surprised that Clare regretted having to leave his birthplace. The severance seems to mark the stage of his first mental derangement. Since those days I have read anything appertaining to Clare with keenest interest, and most of his published poems are in my possession.

The life of John Clare was one of continuous struggle and hardship, pathetic from whatever point of view it may be approached. As most of the details are already known to most people, I have no intention of duplicating them here, except to refute, in the light of new knowledge, much that was exaggerated in those early descriptions of his life.

*Clare's Cottage, Helpstone*
*(Clare's was the end cottage.)*

*Clare Memorial, Helpstone*

The life of John Clare offered so much opportunity for sensational contrast and ridiculous distortion, that it became for many years a favourite subject with writers, each of whom endeavoured to outdo the others in fresh facts about Clare's poverty and mental balance. I remember reading many years ago that drink was the main factor in Clare's mental collapse; 'that Clare pottered in the fields feebly', 'that on his income of £45 a year Clare thought he could live without working'.

The cottage where Clare was born is standing today, almost as it was when he lived there, so that those of my readers who care to do may examine Martin's description of 'a narrow wretched hut more like a prison than a human dwelling' in face of the facts.

When the last published edition of Clare's poems appeared in 1920, Mr Samuel Sefton, of Derby, the grandson of Clare, wrote a biographical sketch for the edition, and he was able to prove many of the distorted notions about Clare to be without the slightest foundation. Even today the district of Helpstone can be seen to hold those simple rural charms that inspired Clare. The lie of the land is such, that effects of light and shade and the changing seasons have full play. It is a country of meadow lands, small woodlands, and winding streams, little rounded hills, with narrow paths where

*Above them hangs the maple tree*
*Below grass swell a velvet hill,*
*And little footpaths sweet to see*
*Go seeking sweeter places still.*

Lord Milton was responsible for securing for Clare a new cottage in the village of Northborough, three miles from Helpstone. Mr Sefton writes: "It was indeed luxurious in comparison with the old stooping house where Clare had spent nearly forty years, but there was more in the old house than mere stone and timber. Clare began to look on the coming change with terror, delayed the move day after day, to the distress of poor Patty; and when at last news came from Milton Park that the Earl was not content with such strange hesitation, and when Patty had her household on the line of march, he 'followed in the rear, walking mechanically with eyes half shut, as if in a dream.'"

*I've left mine own old home of homes,*
*Green fields and every pleasant place.*
*The summer like a stranger comes;*
*I pause and hardly know her face.*
*I miss the hazel's happy green,*
*The bluebell's quiet hanging blooms,*
*Where envy's sneer was never seen,*
*Where staring malice never comes.*

*George's sketch of the memorial*

It seems that Helpstone became a place of some importance during the life of John Clare. Distinguished men of letters and gentry visited the place. On the 9th of March, 1825, Clare wrote in his diary;

'I had a very odd dream last night, and take it as an ill omen … I thought I had one of the proofs of the new poems from London, and after looking at it awhile it shrank through my hand like sand, and crumpled into dust.' Three days afterwards the proof of the *Shepherds Calendar* arrived at Helpstone. The ill omen was to be proved true, but not yet. Clare continued to write and to botanize, and being half forgotten by his earlier friends was contented with the company of two noted local men, Edward Alis, the archaeologist, who discovered ancient Durobrivae (Castor), and Henderson, who assisted Clare in his nature work. These two pleasant companions were in the service of Earl Fitzwilliam. It was perhaps through their interest that Clare weathered the hardships of 1825 so well. Clare died on May 20th 1846.

*George continues:*

The years seem to have passed lightly over Helpstone. Cottages mellowed with age appear to rise naturally out of the soil. Old gardens meet you at every turn, with gnarled apple trees and old world flowers. In the centre of the village is an ancient stone cross, 30 feet in height, and there is also a monument to John Clare.

The church of St Botolph commands immediate attention as one enters the village. Standing upon high ground, it is an ancient building of stone, chiefly in Early English, Decorated and Perpendicular styles, with some traces of Norman work. The lower part of the tower is Norman and stands within the nave. The upper part, including the spire, is Decorated and was rebuilt in 1864. The interesting register dates from the year 1685.

To me the charm of old churches seems to increase with the passing years. It is interesting to look inside on the stonework of an old church to find where the master masons faintly left their signs.

Clare's cottage is still standing and very tastefully restored. To reach it take the turning opposite the Clare Memorial on the main road, next to the post office. Just past the Bluebell Inn you will find Clare's cottage, marked by a commemorative plaque.

So ends our second journey around the county. We hope that you will get as much pleasure from our books as we have had in travelling around and collecting material for them.

Once again we thank the people of Northamptonshire who have given us so much help and assistance. And, of course, we must acknowledge George Harrison, without whose inspiration and vision these two volumes would not have been possible.

A final word from George:

*Reveries*

*Through quiet hours I lie,*
*Denied the boon of restful sleep,*
*Yet strange, those peaceful hours supply*
*More pleasant thoughts than counting sheep.*

*Old scenes, old faces I have known*
*In boyhood days, come back to me,*
*Like scent from flowers strewn*
*Moorlands, blown*
*Above the rolling, restless sea.*

*Sometimes I see a narrow room,*
*With my mother seated there,*
*Her face aglow with healthy bloom,*
*Her kind eyes free from wordly care,*

*And those fond precepts she had thought,*
*And sins are thoughts of yesterday.*

*I live once more those youthful years*
*When hope ran high that I may gain*
*Some honoured place, which man reveres*
*Alas! those dreams have come to nought,*
*Yet aspirations brought the joy*
*Of much of beauty I had sought*
*That future years could not destroy.*

*Thus sleepness hours of night bring peace,*
*For joys outlive the hours of pain*
*The lovely things of life*
*Increase when in our thoughts they live again,*
*If all my nights brought wakeless sleep*
*I would not then known the charm*
*Of drinking from those pleasures deep,*
*That comes through hours of gentle calm.*

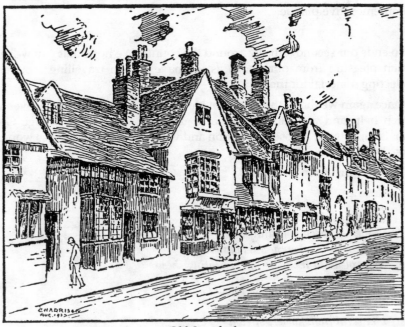

*Old Stamford*

# Index

*The First Breath of Winter*

More about Northamptonshire from Meridian ...

## Wanderers in Northamptonshire
### by John and Vera Worledge

The first part of John and Vera Worledge's tour of the county following in the steps of George Harrison. Covering another forty-seven towns and villages it combines many of the original sketches, poems and articles with present day photographs and descriptive material.
ISBN 1-869922-18-2. £4.95. 112 pages. 53 photographs, 73 drawings. Paperback. 229mm x 145mm.

## Northampton: A guided tour
### by Tony Noble

A comprehensive walking tour of the historic town of Northampton which received its charter from Richard I in 1189.
ISBN 1-869922-06-9. £2.95. 64 pages. 34 photographs. 15 maps. Paperback. A5.

## Exploring Northamptonshire
### by Tony Noble

Twenty trails, each having an historical or geographical theme, which will enable you to explore a county traditionally known for its 'spires and squires'.
Second Edition. ISBN 1-869922-01-8. £4.95. 152 pages. 61 photographs. 24 maps. Paperback. A5.

*Prices correct 1994 but may be subject to revision.*

Available from all booksellers or direct from the Publishers. Please send remittance, adding the following for postage and packing: Order value up to £5.00 add 75p; over £5.00 add £1.00.

**Meridian Books**
**40 Hadzor Road, Oldbury, Warley, West Midlands B68 9LA.**

*Please send s.a.e for our catalogue of books on walking and local history.*